A Parent's Guide To Success For Children

Joann Falciani

Copyright © 2023 **Joann Falciani Publishing**

All rights reserved. No part of this publication may be reproduced, distributed, or transmitted in any form or by any means, including photocopying, recording, or other electronic or mechanical methods, without the prior written permission of the publisher, except in the case of brief quotations embodied in critical reviews and certain other noncommercial uses permitted by copyright law. For permission requests, write to the publisher, addressed "Attention: Book Rights and Permission," at the address below.

Published in the United States of America

ISBN 978-1-960684-74-5 (SC)
ISBN 978-1-960684-73-8 (HC)
ISBN 978-1-960684-14-1 (Ebook)

Joann Falciani Publishing
34 Militia Hill
DrChesterbrook, PA 19087
falcjoann@verizon.net

Ordering Information and Rights Permission:

Quantity sales. Special discounts might be available on quantity purchases by corporations, associations, and others. For details, contact the publisher at the address above.

For Book Rights Adaptation and other Rights Permission. Call us at toll-free 1-888-945-8513 or send us an email at admin@stellarliterary.com.

Contents

CHAPTER 1: How to Choose the Right School for Your Child 1

CHAPTER 2: How to Choose Kindergarten Placement for your Child .. 5

CHAPTER 3: Setting a Routine for Children 9

CHAPTER 4: Why you should choose a Healthy School 13

CHAPTER 5: Teach Children to be Grateful about Holidays 17

CHAPTER 6: Benefits of Sports Participation 19

CHAPTER 7: Parent-Teacher Conflict 21

CHAPTER 8: Family Fun and Staying Safe during Halloween 23

CHAPTER 9: Going Through Divorce 27

CHAPTER 1

How to Choose the Right School for Your Child

Is your child joining Elementary or secondary school? No need to worry we will guide you through each step. It is necessary that you choose a school that suits your child's needs.

It might be a tough and stressful process for you but by following our outlined steps you will find it very easy.

There are many options beyond the public school down the street today. This options leave parents in a confused state over how to make the best decision on which learning environment suits their child best. It is important to know what to look for in a school to ensure your child receives the best possible education for his particular needs.

So, how can you verify if a particular school is capable of meeting your needs? We have come up with some factors you should consider when choosing the best school to provide the right education for your child's specific needs;

Type of school

As a parent you know your child the best therefore you have a responsibility to select the type of school where he or she will thrive and grow. Would your child fare best in a traditional school, a Montessori or a religious affiliated school?

You should also ask questions such as is the academic outcome your main goal? Are you interested in a school that focuses on your Child's unique strengths and weaknesses?

Pupil to teacher ratio

A good school should not have an overcrowded classroom; the proper classroom ratios should be one teacher to six kids for two- year-old kids or one teacher to ten children for preschoolers and Kindergarten. Having too many kids to one teacher will limit the amount of attention the teacher can give to pupils, and nothing is more important at that stage than personalized attention from their teacher.

Proper licensing

A great school will be rightly authorized by the Department of Public Welfare for child care hours and the Department of Education for academic activities. You should call both of these departments to find out if there were any violations marked against the school in the past.

Teacher's credentials

You should verify the credentials and qualifications of your student's teacher; Nearly every state education agency now provides a system that parent's and members of the public can use to check and review the credentials of school teachers in the state.

Make a checklist of relevant questions

Before visiting the school, you should make a list of some important questions to ask the principals and teachers. Some of the essential questions you should ask include:

Verify from the Principals about the staff (teacher) turnover rate.

Ask about their illness policy and when children can return to school after being ill.

You should check out the school playground and find out about the duration of time kids spend outside in different seasons and types of weather.

Inquire about progress reports and communication with the teacher.

Ask about preparation for elementary schools.

Talk to other students and parents if possible to find out necessary details as School staffs are known to put their best foot forward while meeting with potential clients.

CHAPTER 2

How to Choose Kindergarten Placement for your Child

As we start to plan for summer camps for our children, we also need to start evaluating the correct placement for our children who are entering kindergarten. It can be tough to choose whether to hold them back or send them to kindergarten. There are many factors that come into play when making this decision.

The child's birthday: For the children whose birthday's fall between June to August 31, it can be a challenging decision. Parents have to meet with the teacher to see where the child is, not only academically but socially. Is your child a self-starter, can compete one and two set directions?

Independent schools will conduct a placement evaluation to know where the child is and whether the child can attain aca-demic success.

Public schools will also conduct an evaluation, but they are very strict about the August 31st deadline.

If your children have completed a private school kindergarten, they can enter a public school first grade after the school's evaluation.

Boys and girls develop academically and socially at different levels. Boys can benefit from an additional year in the pre-kindergarten and then kindergarten. As a result of this decision, boys will further develop their self-confidence. Since they will be the oldest in the class, they can become leaders.

Girls can also benefit from an additional year in the pre-kindergarten classroom. If their birthday falls towards the end of the summer, they can enter kindergarten and the teacher will evaluate their progress during the year.

This trend is known as "redshirting." It's a term coined for college football players who maintain an extra year of sports eligibility by practicing with the team as freshmen, but not playing in games. The idea of redshirting preschoolers has blossomed in the wake of a 2006 University of California at Santa Barbara study.

Researchers Kathy Bedard and Elizabeth Dhuey found that grade-schoolers who are among the oldest in their class have a distinct competitive learning edge over the youngest kids in their grade, scoring 4 to 12 percent higher on standardized math and science tests.

CHAPTER 3

Setting a Routine for Children

Children thrive when they have a routine and know what is expected of them. Morning drop-off at preschool, along with pick up can be a tough time of the day for both the child and parents. As adults, we need to include our children in the process.

Here are a few tips:

1) Children should have a healthy breakfast at home before leaving for school. This allows the child to get some energy and prevent eating breakfast at school.
2) Children should carry their own belongings such as backpacks, and lunches to school. Allow children to put away their own belongings. This allows the child to build independence, as well as establishing the routine of drop off.
3) The drop off should be quick. When parents linger at school, the child becomes confused and thinks the parents are staying.
4) There should be either a quick hug, kiss or a wave at the window.
5) Parents should tell the child they will always come back after work.

Model social graces of greeting the teacher in the morning as well as your child greeting the teacher.

Please arrive early. When children arrive late, children can get anxious if they walk in and all the children are looking at them while circle time is being held.

Talk to your child about all the exciting activities that go on at school. Talk about math and playing on the playground. Allow your child to tell you what they love about school.

The teacher can assist with the drop off by greeting the child with a smile and enthusiasm as the child arrives.

Pick up time should have a routine. Children should gather their own belongings and prepare to go home. Parents should have a short chat about their child's day. This is not the time for a parent conference. Teachers are watching other children and can't have lengthy conversations. Parents must refrain from being on the phone during drop off and pick up. Parents should not be distracted by a phone call and should put all their attention on their child and setting them up for a successful day.

The important message is just like adults, children need to know what the expectations are of them, and they will rise to the occasion.

CHAPTER 4

Why you should choose a Healthy School

It's the end of Winter and Spring is approaching, we are reminded that children and teachers are more prone to getting sick with variety odd illnesses which include the flu, strep and common cold.

As a parent, a call from the school can be both frustrating and concerning. You have to leave work and possibly stay home for a couple days.

Here are some tips from a Washington Post Article about keeping everybody healthy:

When a child seems sick or the rash comes on suddenly, a trip to the doctor might be wise, said Linda Davis-Alldritt, a registered nurse and the president of the National Association of School Nurses.

The Common Cold

Stuffy noses, low-grade fevers and coughs are fine as long as the symptoms are mild, the student can do her work and she is not disturbing her classmates.

"By the time symptoms manifest, the child has likely already become contagious," Devore said. "Most kids and teachers are exposed to common viruses, including cold viruses, regularly.

There are enough viruses to have a fresh cold every week and still have a normal immune system."

Influenza

Stay home! Signs that your child has the flu and not a common cold include higher fever, aches and pains, fatigue and severe cough.

"With flu, the fever can be 102 or even higher," Davis-Alldritt said.

"You can look at your kids and you can tell when they are really sick."

Eye discharge

Conjunctivitis, or pink eye, is just that: eye discharge paired with pink or red in the whites of the eyes. It can be caused by a virus or bacteria, or by dust or allergens. The viral and bacterial versions are contagious.

"It's very hard to differentiate between allergic eye irritation and an infection," Davis-Alldritt said. "If as a parent you think it's pinkeye, it's a good idea to call their health-care provider."

Sore throat

Sometimes it's strep. Sometimes it's just irritation from a cold or other respiratory infection. If it's not severe and not accompanied by a significant fever, a child can go to school. If it is strep, she will need to stay home until after she has been on antibiotics for a full day and is feeling better, Devore said. For a viral sore throat, a child should stay home until she has been fever-free for 24 hours.

Vomiting and diarrhea

There's very little gray area here. If your child is throwing up or has diarrhea, the child needs to be picked up from school and kept at home for twenty-four hours. This rule keeps everyone healthy.

Prevention

Kids can prevent many common illnesses with a few simple steps: frequently washing hands for at least 20 seconds with soap and warm water; coughing and sneezing into their elbows; keeping their hands away from their eyes and face; and getting a flu shot and keeping other vaccines up-to-date.

We as educators and parents need to keep everybody healthy and work together for the best interest of the child. The important message is a child doesn't need a fever to be sick. If the child can't perform in the daily activities at school, he needs to stay home, and receive some medication.

CHAPTER 5

Teach Children to be Grateful about Holidays

As I sit in my living room with my tree, lights and wrapping paper. I can't help to think it is truly a magical time of year especially as a teacher of preschoolers. Children are excited in anticipation of Christmas morning and all the magic it brings. Nowadays, Children are also learning to appreciate and embrace several cultures and learn about Hanukkah and Kwanza. We also have a responsibility to teach children the true meaning of Christmas and the joy of giving as well as doing for others.

Here are a few helpful hints to teach children about the joy of the holidays.

1. We can teach children about how to be grateful for everything they have and how they can give to others. Children can help out others, get them involved. Children can go into the community to pass out Christmas cookies and a small message of hope. This will help teach them how to be loving and giving and that the holidays are not all about getting but about helping others.
2. Saint Nicholas Day is a wonderful opportunity to have children choose three or four toys that they don't play with me anymore and give them away to a shelter or a community center.
3. Children can make holiday cards and drawings and visit a senior center to drop them off for the residents.
4. The biggest lesson we can teach children this time of year is about how to make wonderful memories. Spend time with your children and do some fun activities such as:

Bake cookies

Watch a holiday movie as a family with popcorn.

Take a day trip to see Christmas lights Longwood gardens,

Read a holiday book

Make ornaments

CHAPTER 6

Benefits of Sports Participation

We are packing up the beach towels and putting away the bathing suits for the season, fall sports have started for children across the area. Sports have multiple benefits for children on and off the field. Participation in sports can build children's self-esteem as well as their self -confidence. Sports also teaches children goal setting and the importance of following through.

Children gain the following skills:

Social Skills

Sports participation will help children in developing skills that will last a lifetime. They learn to play with children in the same age bracket as well as older children who can act as a role models. Children learn leadership skills, communication and social skills, and grace that they can carry over in their adulthood.

Self-Esteem

Children's self-esteem will increase as they get praise for a job well done. They also learn outshine themselves and reach their athletic potential by the encouragement from coaches. Children also learn to accept constructive criticism which is also an important skill.

School Success

Children who participate in sports excel in academics. They apply the same dedication and hard work on and off the field. Children also are more confident and learn to manage their time better which is a life-long skill.

Health

Children who actively engage in sports also make health food choices. Sports is an excellent way to encourage healthy habit which we should instill in our young ones to carry over to adulthood.

CHAPTER 7

Parent-Teacher Conflict

The relationship between teachers and parents is important to the success of the child at school. Parents will have concerns and issues throughout the school year. Here are some helpful tips to help resolve and navigate these conflicts:

1. In a preschool, drop off and pick up is not always the best time to discuss an in-depth issue with the teacher. Rather, ask for a time to meet or talk during the day that is convenient for both of you.
2. As a parent, you can email the teacher to briefly discuss an issue, but a face to face meeting is more appropriate to resolve an issue.
3. As parents, remember the school and the parents are a team and both want the best for the child.
4. Teachers need to remain objective and use positive words when they discuss the challenges for the child.
5. As a teacher, you need to listen to parents and validate their concern. Parents want to be heard and getting the best for their child is their paramount objective.
6. The parents need to be aware their child is not the only child in the class, and sometimes they should offer advice to the child of how to become a problem solver.

The school and parents are a team who need to work together to provide children with a safe and nurturing environment.

CHAPTER 8

Family Fun and Staying Safe during Halloween

Can you feel it already? Another October 31st is here and Its Halloween season!

Halloween is one of the most exciting and anticipated holidays in the United States, second only to Christmas. It presents such an exciting time for the family to get together for some fun activities; but for the kids, it's like magic in the air! It's that time of the year when they get to wear spooky costumes, enjoy parties and roam the neighborhood looking for treats.

The list of activities for the perfect Halloween must include Family activities and don't forget the ancient tradition of "trick or treat." There are lots of fun activities that the whole family will enjoy on Halloween day, and we have listed a couple of them for you to choose from, any of the activities on this list is guaranteed to give your Halloween celebration a buzz that you won't forget in a long time.

1. Halloween is a great time to go apple picking with the whole family. Who doesn't like apples? You could visit any of the local orchards such as Highland Orchards, Linville orchards or Milky Way Farms. While there, you could also pick pumpkins to carve while munching on some apple cider doughnuts.
2. You could also get some brown or white paper bags to make Halloween lanterns. Just get a small powered tea lamp and a string, and you are good to go!
3. You could design and craft home-made trick or treat bags and also have the children adorn themselves in their Halloween costumes, masks, and paints.
4. You could buy Halloween cookie cutters and have everyone sit around the dining table and make cookies with Halloween themes.
5. Another excellent activity idea is to make Halloween Candy popcorns for the whole family.
6. You could also use the pumpkin seeds to make amazing Halloween crafts like necklaces and paper plates.
7. Later in the evening just before it gets dark, you could all make toilet paper ghosts and put up Halloween decorations

During the evening

As soon as it starts getting dark, it's time for the kids to go out for trick or treat, and in the midst of the euphoria; it is easy for them to let loose and abandon safety precautions. For parents, you can follow these simple tips to keep your children safe during trick or treat:

1. For younger children aged below 7 years, they should be accompanied by at least one adult. For older children, they should go out in pairs.
2. They should follow a planned route and can only go to houses with a well-lit porch
3. Take care to decorate the kid's costumes and bags with reflective tape or stickers and, if possible, choose light colors as this will increase their visibility in the dark.
4. Endeavor to use paints instead of masks which can obstruct a child's vision and make it harder to see oncoming vehicles.
5. Also, have kids carry glow sticks or flashlights to help them see and be seen by drivers and when selecting a costume, make sure it is the right size to pre- vent trips and falls.

CHAPTER 9

Going Through Divorce

Children are human sponges and will absorb and process information very well when explained in a simple and concise manner. We need to be aware of their ability to process a great deal of information all at once. The subject of divorce is no different and needs to be handled with a great deal of reassurance. They should know that the divorce is not their fault.

Here are some tips to on how to have a discussion with your children about divorce when it occurs:

1. Reassure your children they will still see both parents. Both mom and dad still love them and will always be there for them.
2. They will have two houses where they can play, sleep and have friends over.
3. Parents of young children should maintain routines, provide consistency in rules and expectations, and provide extra affection. Provide young children with repeated reassurances that the divorce is not their fault and that you love them.

Children will ask many questions about the divorce and how it will affect them day to day. Their schedule will change. The child needs to understand that they will spend time with each parent, just not together. As a parent you should seek help from a professional when needed. The professional will be objective, and your children may feel more comfortable talking to a professional, rather than you.

The school is also an important factor in helping children handle divorce and their situation. With so many changes in their schedule, the children will look to the school as a place that provides stability and support. We as educators should listen to the children, but also set limits on behaviors that are acceptable.

We need to let children know that they are valued through our smiles and positive feedback for their efforts as well as their progress. Many children say they do not want to be pitied, but they do want to hear about what they do well. Give them opportunities for leadership and to help the teacher as well as their classmates.

Divorce is a challenge for both the parents and children. Both school and parents need to reassure the children that they are loved and safe. As adults, we need to only say positive qualities about each other because children internalize their feelings and can act based on what they have heard and seen. The best recipe is to make sure children feel safe and loved.

Thank You for Reading Our Book! ©

Printed by Libri Plureos GmbH in Hamburg, Germany